Let My People Know...
and Go

Frontier Mission
of the
Presbyterian Church (USA)

Let My People Know... and Go

Frontier Mission of the Presbyterian Church (USA)

Edited by
Jennifer L. Pratt
Tom Theriault
Judy Theriault

Presbyterian Center for Mission Studies
Pasadena, California, USA

Additional copies of this book may be ordered from:

The Presbyterian Center for Mission Studies
1605 E. Elizabeth Street
Pasadena, California 91104
USA

Phone: (818) 398-2468
FAX: (818) 398-2391
e-mail: pcms.parti@ecunet.org

© 1996 by The Presbyterian Center for Mission Studies
Printed in the United States of America
Library of Congress Catalog Card Number: 96-68906
ISBN 0-9652533-0-9
Cover photos by Richard Satterlee

Table of Contents

Let My People Know... and Go

Table of Contents (continued)

Zoque women and child
  Photo courtesy of Westminster Presbyterian Church,
                              Yakima

Let My People Know... and Go

List of Photos

Let My People Know... and Go

List of Photos (continued)

Let My People Know... and Go

List of Illustrations
Illustrations by Ruth Elliott

Oromo woman of Ethiopia   *Photo by Judy Theriault*

Let My People Know... and Go

ix

Acknowledgments

Presbyterian Center for Mission Studies
Research and Promotion Team:

Editor: Jennifer L. Pratt

Copy Editors: Tom Theriault
Judy Theriault
Beth Venn
Steve Pratt

Staff Writers: Tom Theriault
Jennifer Pratt
Jeff Hamm
Judy Theriault
Barbara Lewis
Cathy Witte

Research Assistants: Phyllis Sewell
Frances May

Cover Photos: Richard Satterlee

Illustrations: Ruth Elliott

Layout Artist: Steve Simpson

Let My People Know... and Go

Thank you!

"Thank you" to the many people who volunteered time and energy to help us complete this project. To those of you who provided much needed information... to those of you who sent wonderful pictures (see List of Photos)... to those of you who corrected dozens of pages of manuscript... and to the Presbyterian Frontier Fellowship staff and the staff of the International Evangelism Office, Presbyterian Church (USA)... you are all greatly appreciated! *Thank you!*

As we send this book to press, we pray that Jesus Christ will be lifted up through our efforts and that the Holy Spirit will speak through the words and pictures that follow.

Let us, the Presbyterian Church (USA), pick up the banner of Christ, join Christians around the globe, and go forward into the world, proclaiming God's love to all peoples. May we take courage and be bold! May we speak out and speak up! May we go... go... with God as our Guide. There is much to learn, much to see, much to do... and much cause for rejoicing. Are you ready? *Let's GO!!*

...and may all praise, honor and glory be to our Lord Jesus Christ, now and forever!

Jennifer L. Pratt
for the Presbyterian Center for Mission Studies
Pasadena, California, USA

Let My People Know... and Go

To Know IS to Go!—*Introduction*

"I want my life to count; I want my church to count." The world is a big place and so much of what happens is out of our control. It is easy to feel insignificant, with the result that we tend to turn inward, focusing on our own problems and pleasures. But the FACT is that you and your church can play a strategic role in the most earth-shaking undertaking of all.

It's true, the world IS a big place. But we know a far BIGGER God who has a thrilling plan for this sin-sick world, a plan that will get us up and on the go! Our Lord's Prayer is not just wishful thinking: His Kingdom will come, His will will be done on earth. The Savior will return and fully establish His reign of peace and righteousness, and we have a pivotal part to play in that coming Kingdom. According to Jesus, that grand day will not dawn until "the Gospel of the Kingdom is preached throughout the whole world as a testimony to every culture and tribe" (Matthew 24:14).

Knowing God's love and plan for the world, our Presbyterian forebears got going! Along with countless other faithful disciples, they have planted a vital outpost of the Kingdom (a church) in about half the world's ethnic clusters. So the job Jesus left for us to do is about half done! Visionary Christians the world over are rallying around a stretching challenge: could it be possible, in the foreseeable future, to plant a winning witness for Christ in each of the world's 10,000 still unreached people groups? With the head-spinning advances of communication and transportation, and with the astounding missionary forces being raised up in the "two-thirds world," many are asserting that "we can do it if we will do it!"

Not to be left out, the 1991 General Assembly officially embraced this history-shaping cause: "The Presbyterian Church (USA) is claiming the evangelistic task afresh! ...particularly among

Let My People Know... and Go

xii

unreached people groups..." ("Turn to the Living God"). Flowing from this mission manifesto is the challenge to congregations to "adopt" one of these unreached people groups, making a wholehearted commitment to get to know and pray for the group until a viable church is established in its midst. Our Presbyterian version of this "adopt-a-people" approach is called "Commitment to Share Good News." It ideally suits smaller or larger churches, any body of Christians who will simply but powerfully care about a tribe or culture which has yet to experience the saving love of Christ. As you know a people group, then God can direct you to Go—in *prayer*, in *person*, through your *pocketbook*, or through any number of other strategic avenues of involvement.

One New Testament scholar has written:

> "What the Church does with the Gospel is more important than the march of armies or the actions of the world's capitals, because it is in the accomplishment of this mission that the divine purpose for human history is accomplished. Let us be done with any inferiority complex... [for we can participate] in God's plan for the ages."
> (G.E. Ladd in The Gospel of the Kingdom)

We American Presbyterians must do our part. Knowing the love and plan of Christ for the world, will we get going? In the following pages you will meet a sampling of the eighty unreached people groups to which the PC(USA) currently supports outreach efforts. It is our denomination's goal that Presbyterians will be engaged in ministry among 200 such groups by the year 2000. And so, empowered by the Holy Spirit, we plan to grow! We hope this book will help you grow in frontier mission vision and involvement by:

1) providing information which will allow you and/or your church to intelligently choose and commit

Let My People Know... and Go

to an unreached group;

2) supplying inspiration for regular prayer for our Presbyterian frontier mission ministries.

Will you and your church join history-shaping Christians around the world and make a commitment to a specific people group? As you read and pray for the groups we are ministering among, let the Holy Spirit speak to you as to the strategic part you can play in the most significant venture on the planet. Don't you agree?

To Know *is to GO!*

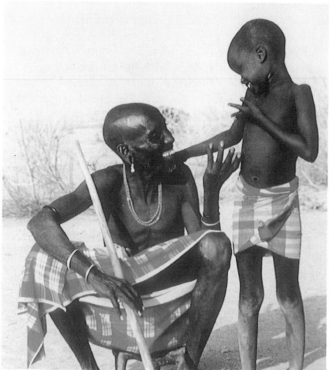

Rendille man and boy of Kenya   *Photo courtesy of Wycliffe Bible Translators, International*

Let My People Know... and Go

Stepping In—*The Challenge*

Are you ready?
You are on the verge of a journey that could change your life and that of your church.

Think big! Expect exciting things!

The God of Abraham, Isaac, Jacob...
of Sarah, Rebekah and Rachel...
The God of the Yup'ik, Zoque, Surma ...
of the Mamprusi, Dalits and Kurds...
desires to introduce you to the people groups still
unreached today.

May you see these peoples through God's eyes and with God's heart. May you be blessed as you come to know them. With your knowledge and prayers, may you be a blessing to them in return.

We have included a Bible study in the back of this book that attempts to sketch out God's plan to draw all peoples to Himself. It is our hope that it will provide valuable insight to complement the "people stories" and provoke new realizations concerning God's WORD for the WORLD.

Also, the last section of this book, "Stepping Out—An Invitation to Get Involved," provides a "road map" useful in the continuation of your journey out into the world, with God as your Guide.

"...I tell you, open your eyes and look at the fields..." John 4:35

Are you ready?

Let My People Know... and Go

GOOOOOOAAAAAAAALLLL!!!!!! If you watched or listened to a broadcast of the 1994 World Cup soccer tournament in Los Angeles, you heard this distinctive victory cry.

The Arabic-Speaking Muslims of Southern California

The Arabic Communication Center (ACC) rejoiced over God's victory during their World Cup Outreach. Many of the Arabic-speaking Muslims, who attended the soccer games, heard a personal witness of the Gospel and responded with a profession of new faith in the Savior. Many more around the globe saw the ACC's television programs which highlighted the World Cup events coupled with Christian testimonies from Arabic-speaking athletes. The series, entitled "Who Will Win?" introduced viewers to the ultimate victor, Jesus Christ. The ACC produces both radio and television programs to proclaim the Gospel to Arabic-speaking people in the Middle East and around the world. It also sponsors Bible studies and other events designed for Arabic-speaking Muslims in Southern California.

Who are the Arabic-Speaking Muslims of Southern California?

There are over 350,000 Arabic-speaking people in the Los Angeles area. Most come from Lebanon, Egypt and Syria and live in and around Pasadena, Glendale, and North Hollywood. The majority of the Arab-speaking people in Southern California are Muslims.

Los Angeles has one of the largest concentrations of Muslims in the USA and is quickly becoming a major political and cultural center for the Arab community. There are twenty-two Arabic-speaking congregations in the Los Angeles area, but the churches are small and most of their pastors hold secular jobs in addition to their pastoral duties. Most of these churches minister primarily to Arabic-speaking Christians who experienced persecution from the Muslim majority in their homelands. Evangelism of Arabic-speaking Muslims is not a high priority for most of the Christians in these churches. But God has raised up other messengers to proclaim the Good News to those who have not heard.

Presbyterian Involvement

Dr. Hisham Kamel, a Presbyterian pastor from Egypt, now residing in Southern California, heads the Arabic Communication Center (ACC) and works tirelessly with the goal of enabling every person in the Arab world to hear the Good News at least once. Presbyterians are partnering with Dr. Kamel and the ACC in two ways. The ACC's local outreach has become a new church development in the San Gabriel Presbytery and is growing in numbers and vitality. This new church uses creative means to invite Arabic-speaking Muslims to seeker–friendly events and Bible studies and it works to inspire Arabic-speaking Christians to share their faith with Muslims.

The Presbyterian Frontier Mission Fund helps to

Let My People Know... and Go

Dr. Hisham Kamel reading for film production
Photo courtesy of Arabic Communication Center

support the international outreach of the ACC by
contributing to the costs of media production and
broadcasting. Rapid proliferation of satellite disks,
radios, and televisions both here and abroad has put
the world's 203 million Arabic-speaking people within
reach. The response has been excellent. The ACC sends
Bibles to those who request them and often times has
far more requests than they can fill. They wait upon
the Lord and regularly take giant steps of faith
expecting that God will provide the needed resources.
God has repeatedly provided in amazing and
miraculous ways.

The 1994 World Cup outreach was a strategic effort
to get the attention of Arabic-speaking sports fans who
tuned in for news of their teams competing in world
class events. News of the winners in sports was
combined with news of Jesus Christ, the cosmic victor.
Now the ACC is planning another outreach to coincide
with the 1996 Olympics in Atlanta. Let us help the

Let My People Know... and Go

Arabic Communication Center "Go for the Gold," in the race to bring Arabic-speaking people to a saving knowledge of Jesus Christ.

Prayer Concerns

PLEASE PRAY without ceasing for:
- the Immanuel Bible Study held weekly at the ACC.
- local Arabic churches to increase their support of the ACC and for their participation in local outreach to Muslims.
- the Holy Spirit to work in the hearts of the people listening to and watching the ACC productions both in the USA and across the Arab world.

Vital Statistics

Religion
Islam
Language
Arabic, English
Population
Arabs in Southern California: 350,000+
USA*: 258,204,000
Christian Status
(includes Protestants, Catholics, Orthodox)
Arabs in Southern California: Unknown
USA*: 86.5%

*Note: includes all people groups

"God kept us safe"...

The Southeast Asian Refugees of Fresno, California

"God kept us safe
day after day, as it got harder to hold
holding on to our hopes and dreams
to a place of a whole new beginning
crossing the Mekong to the San Joaquin
not knowing the danger we'd have to face
for the days in our life...
traveled for such a long time to the San Joaquin
navigating across the Mekong
like a war zone
seeing family members gunned down by army
soldiers
relating to gangs in the San Joaquin
killing and stealing...
but God reached out to us..."
-excerpt from poem entitled "From Mekong to
San Joaquin River,"
by Nikone Chomphosy, age 16

Who are the Southeast Asian Refugees of Fresno, California?

There are over 60,000 southeast Asian refugees in Fresno. Fleeing their countries to escape persecution and turbulent political and economic conditions, these people have settled in the Fresno area where climate and farmland are much like their homelands. Hmong, Laotian, Cambodian, Vietnamese, Mien, and many more peoples have arrived in the USA, looking for a sure foundation upon which to rear their families.

Making the transition to life in the USA is not easy. Refugees struggle to preserve their cultural identity and, at the same time, to fit into their new American environment. Commonly, they experience fear and insecurity. They feel disconnected from their familiar traditions and from the culture of the new world. With opportunities limited, most refugees find themselves living in poverty.

A Firm Foundation

The greater Fresno community has watched as their city has taken new shape. Many Christians have seen the changes as a chance to welcome and love the strangers in their land (Leviticus 19:33-34). Rev. Sharon Stanley of the PC(USA) and Rev. Bounkham Nounvilaythong of the American Baptist Church coordinate the Fresno Interdenominational Refugee Ministries (FIRM). The purpose of FIRM is to demonstrate and proclaim Christ's love and to encourage relationships between refugee and American communities.

A local TV series featured one of FIRM's ministries through University Presbyterian Church, "God's Asian Youth Group." According to member Nip Chomphosy, "You can stay in your gang and still come to our youth group. But you can't do bad stuff in your gang while you're in this group." Having found Jesus Christ to be her eternal Savior and friend, Nip is busy inviting people to church, that they might discover the same truth.

Let My People Know... and Go

Members of God's Asian Youth Group

Photo courtesy of FIRM

The Presbyterian frontier mission ministry is supporting FIRM. Dave Hackett, General Director of Presbyterian Frontier Fellowship, reports that Christians in Fresno are welcoming the refugees as they would welcome Jesus Himself. They are coaching the city through a difficult time and, Dave says, "Along the way, they are showing that the firm foundation of Jesus Christ is a foundation that people from any race and culture can stand on — giving them faith in themselves and in the redeeming God."

Prayer Concerns

PLEASE PRAY without ceasing that:
* there will be a continued reduction in crime and violence in the Fresno area.
* God will provide the directors of FIRM with wisdom and energy.
* God will raise up volunteers and provide contributions to keep the ministry alive.

Let My People Know... and Go

Vital Statistics

Religion Buddhism, Confucianism
Language Hmong, Laotian, Cambodian, Vietnamese, Mien, Khmu
Population S.E. Asians in Fresno: 60,000 USA*: 258,204,000
Christian Status (includes Protestants, Catholics, Orthodox) S.E. Asians in Fresno : 5% USA*: 86.5%

*Note: includes all people groups

Summer Youth Program (FIRM) serving children
Photo courtesy of FIRM

Let My People Know... and Go

Ekwoot Preeyagrysorn, or "Woot," is a descendant of one of the three original martyrs of the first Christian fellowship established in Thailand over 120 years ago...

The Thai of Chicago, Illinois

Now living in the USA, Ekwoot has been attending the Thai Presbyterian Fellowship of Chicago. With the departure of their pastor in July of 1994, Woot has become the chairperson for the small congregation. Working at Sharp Electronics Company as a technician, he says that he "can only work on the church work from

Lay Leader Ekwoot Preeyagrysorn

Photo by Dave Hackett

Let My People Know... and Go

9 p.m. to midnight, five days a week, plus Saturday Bible studies and the preparation of the bulletin and then the meetings and worship on Sunday." He says that, "God is asking him to do it [become a pastor] and I've always said, 'No, it's not me.' But this time I know God is calling me." (Taken from an interview done by Dave Hackett of Presbyterian Frontier Fellowship.)

Opportunities Outside Thailand

Thailand is 98 percent Buddhist. There are still high social barriers against conversion throughout the land. God continues to guide and bless ministry efforts in Thailand. He is also reaching the Thai, however, outside their homeland.

The Thai Presbyterian Fellowship

The Thai Presbyterian Fellowship of Chicago draws from all over the Chicago area, as well as from Wisconsin and Illinois. The people meet every Sunday afternoon for worship at the Filipino Community Presbyterian Church. The Filipino church, under the leadership of the Rev. Daniel Arciaga, has allowed the Thai fellowship to use their facilities, and Rev. Arciaga has offered to train the elders and provide emergency pastoral care.

The Thai fellowship was organized to target Asian-Americans, especially of Thai origin. Members take turns holding Bible studies in their homes. After worship on Sundays the people come together for fellowship. They also offer classes for children and young adults to learn about the Thai culture and language.

There are 60,000 Thai people in Chicago. Although there are only 20 to 30 regular members of the Thai Presbyterian Fellowship, we can expect God to do a great work through them in reaching the Thai community with a culturally sensitive presentation of the Gospel that speaks to their unique needs as immigrants adjusting to life in a new country.

Prayer Concerns

PLEASE PRAY without ceasing for:
- additional full-time pastors to assist in leading and expanding the Thai Fellowship in Chicago and throughout the country.
- increased financial support to undergird the Thai Fellowship.
- guidance and support for Ekwoot as he pursues the Lord's call on his life.

Vital Statistics

Religion
Buddhism
Language
Thai, English
Population
Thai in Chicago: 60,000
USA*: 258,204,000
Christian Status
(includes Protestants, Catholics, Orthodox)
Thai in Chicago: 0.5%
USA*: 86.5%

*Note: includes all people groups

The Holy Spirit is on the move...

The Eastern Oromo

Hararge Outreach

The Ethiopian Evangelical Church Mekane Yesus (EECMY), our partner church in Ethiopia, is moving with the Spirit. From the Hararge (Harar District), east of Addis Ababa, come reports of God's work: a man born blind receives sight; a boy with rabies and a man with epilepsy are healed; and with each miracle, families—sometimes whole villages—are coming to faith in the Great Physician, Jesus Christ.

Nothing Impossible with God

The Oromo practiced their traditional form of worship for centuries before Islam was brought to the region. Today most Oromo in the Hararge would call themselves Muslim, but are unfamiliar with the Koran and combine traditional beliefs with those of Islam. Early Christian missionary efforts proved unsuccessful, but this is a new day. Realizing that the Great Commission commands us to go, and believing that nothing is impossible with God, the EECMY began a new evangelistic effort in the Harar area.

God's Work

With funding from the PC(USA) Frontier Mission Fund, seven Ethiopian evangelists were sent out in the fall of 1994. It is mainly through their ministry of prayer and preaching that God is working in

Let My People Know... and Go

Rev. Berhano Ofgaa and Rev. Mezgebu Fufa, directors of outreach in the Hararge   *Photo by Judy Theriault*

extraordinary ways. Property is hard to obtain in Ethiopia, and the church is required to begin social programs such as schools or clinics in order to qualify to buy land. Then they may build a church as well. With their limited financial resources, the EECMY has only recently been able to establish its first church in the Harar province, but God is providing other ways. The Catholic Church, whose twenty-two-year-old mission in the area has produced little fruit, has recognized the hand of the Lord on the EECMY efforts, and plans to withdraw and turn their property over to the newcomers.

God is also on the move, bringing good from the hardships resulting from the former Marxist regime. A few years ago governmental policies forced many Ethiopians to resettle in the towns of their birth. Trauma and economic hardship resulted, but the diaspora also transplanted Christians from other parts of the country back into the Muslim region of Harar. Their presence is providing stability and support for the new outreach.

Rev. Iteffa Gobena, Director of Evangelism for the
Ethiopian Evangelical Church Mekane Yesus, with an
Oromo family   *Photo by Judy Theriault*

Prayer Concerns

PLEASE PRAY without ceasing for:
- more training opportunities for evangelists and
  finances to deploy them. It costs about $2,000 to
  support an evangelist for one year.
- new believers who often suffer persecution from the
  Muslim population and the Orthodox Church, which
  in Ethiopia, combines elements of Christianity with

Let My People Know... and Go

traditional beliefs.
- poor farmers to find a replacement crop for "chat" which is an addictive drug and the backbone of the local economy. Through prayer, addicts are being healed and coming to faith in Christ.
- the planned transfer of the Catholic property to the EECMY to go smoothly, and for other windfalls of blessing for God's people. (Because the Muslims receive financial help from the Middle East they have no trouble underwriting social services, land purchases and mosque construction.) Pray that the church of Jesus Christ will grow in spite of the competition.

Vital Statistics

Religion   Islam, Traditional
Language   Oromo

Population
     Hararge Oromo: 2,200,000
     Ethiopia*: 52,569,000

Christian Status
     (includes Protestants, Catholics, Orthodox)
       Hararge Oromo: < 1%
       Ethiopia*: 58%

*Note: includes all people groups

Twice a week the Kalicha's compound fills with men and women who come to spend the night dancing amid incense and drum beats inviting the spirits to come...

The Shekicho

Shekicho boys   *Photo by Judy Theriault*

Let My People Know... and Go

The Shekicho believe in one creator god and many lesser deities, ancestor spirits, whom they fear and work hard to appease with the hope of gaining favor and forgiveness. Their rituals include blood sacrifices, usually goats and chickens. On special occasions a bull is offered, and some families have even sacrificed their children. The Kalicha, or local witch doctor, is believed to be indwelt by powerful spirits, and he makes his living by charging fees for the spells, curses and remedies he offers. But recently some of the witch doctors have found their business dwindling, and a few have been forced to pack up and move elsewhere, looking for a more lucrative following. Why the change? Some Shekicho have found something better. Nearly five thousand have come to faith in Jesus Christ!

God is at Work

Years ago Presbyterian missionaries attempted to plant churches among the Shekicho in the jungles and rain forests of western Ethiopia. But until recently the Shekicho showed little interest in the Savior. Five years ago the Illubabor Bethel Synod of the Ethiopian Evangelical Church Mekane Yesus (EECMY) began several preaching places in Shekicho territory. Currently, pastors from other areas take turns preaching at these outposts. God is at work, and new churches are sprouting. But because each is made up entirely of newborn believers it needs careful discipling.

EECMY has High Hopes

The EECMY has plans to expand their outreach geographically, and to provide additional services to

Let My People Know... and Go

Ato Mersha, synod president, stands in front of one of three Shekicho churches   *Photo by Judy Theriault*

benefit the Shekicho. Less than two percent of the population can read, and they have no written language of their own. Almost every Shekicho person suffers from a preventable disease resulting from poor diet, polluted water or lack of basic sanitation. The leaders of the EECMY are moving forward in faith expecting God to provide the resources needed. Their goal is to show the Shekicho that, rather than living in fear they can rejoice in the love and power of the one true God.

Prayer Concerns

PLEASE PRAY without ceasing for:
- safety and boldness for those who are challenging the control of the spirits and Kalichas. Ask Jesus to display his power over the evil spirits so that more Shekicho will come to believe in Him.
- Pastor Lucas Gerbre, a Shekicho who has been to

Let My People Know... and Go

Bible school and now ministers among his people. He is the only ordained Shekicho and the only church leader who speaks the language. Most outreach is done through translators. Pray that God would use him mightily and that other Christian leaders will emerge from the Shekicho.

- the churches that are made up entirely of new believers. They have only occasional help from mature Christians. They need Scripture in their own language and they need to learn to read and follow it. Pray for a Bible translator and resources to underwrite translation and literacy work.

Vital Statistics

Religion   Traditional
Language   Shekicho

Population
    Shekicho: 110,000
    Ethiopia*: 52,569,000

Christian Status
    (includes Protestants, Catholics, Orthodox)
    Shekicho: 4%
    Ethiopia*: 58%

*Note: includes all people groups

Let My People Know... and Go

In the mountainous area of Southwest Ethiopia, sometimes known as the Alps of Africa, the Surma people make their home...

The Surma

Bargola, the first Surma believer

Photo by Judy Theriault

Let My People Know... and Go

The Surma of Ethiopia, Africa

The Surma are a proud semi-nomadic people who are known for their unique practice of measuring their women's beauty by the striking lip plates which they wear. The rich Surma culture also includes body painting and the donga, a stick fighting competition in which men prove their manhood, resolve quarrels, and bring honor to the village. The Surma are proud of their culture and are resistant to change, especially when it is suggested from the outside.

Who are the Surma?

The Surma are herders and farmers. Their diet consists of milk and blood from their cattle, augmented with agricultural produce. Recently, famine, intertribal warfare with the Bomi peoples, and resulting cattle raids, have caused displacement among the Surma.

To date the Surma have no indigenous church, and only two of the 40,000 Surma have accepted Jesus Christ as their Savior. Most Surma hold to their traditional religion and believe in a supreme being called Tumu.

God's Work

Presbyterian missionary work began in Ethiopia in 1919. Today, we partner with the Ethiopian Evangelical Church Mekane Yesus (EECMY). Two Presbyterian missionaries, John and Gwen Haspels, work among the Surma.

John and Gwen are striving to bring these people to a knowledge of Jesus Christ through their long-term presence and holistic witness—helping the Surma to meet their needs for food, livestock, roads, health care and education.

Let My People Know... and Go

Left to right are Stephanos—bookkeeper and evangelist, Bargola—linguist and translator, Jibril Abmed—translator, and John Haspels—PC(USA) missionary   *Photo by Judy Theriault*

Although the Surma are resistant to change, the recent cultural upheaval and the Haspels' presence is likely to encourage an acceptance and spread of the Gospel. The Haspels report that in some tribal decisions the Surma are considering what the Christian God expects of them. This is an exciting first step toward bringing glory to God. God is indeed working amidst the Surma!

Prayer Concerns

PLEASE PRAY without ceasing that:
- the Surma's eyes will be opened to the truth of the Gospel.
- there will be peace between the Surma and their neighbors.
- the Haspels may gain the trust and friendship of the Surma and that their relationships may bring the Surma to acknowledge their Creator.
- the team working with the Surma will be protected in every way and strengthened for the intense spiritual warfare that they experience. May they be blessed with, and enabled to demonstrate, unity and

Holy Spirit power as they work to translate Scripture and show the love of Jesus.
- the first Surma believer (pictured) may grow in righteousness and boldness in his witness for Christ.

Vital Statistics

Religion	
	Traditional
Language	
	Surma
Population	
	Surma: 40,000
	Ethiopia*: 52,569,000
Christian Status	
	(includes Protestants, Catholics, Orthodox)
	Surma: 0%
	Ethiopia*: 58%

*Note: includes all people groups

Reaching the Peoples Who Have Never Heard...

The Northern Outreach Programme

"Living Waters Cesspool Co." "Beautiful Savior Hair Salon." Signs such as these dot the landscape and witness to the spread of the Gospel in southern Ghana. But, Christians recognized a startling imbalance. Whereas 34 percent of the Ghanian population lives in the less developed north, only 3 percent of the Christian workers and 2 percent of church funds were being used to reach the predominantly non-Christian tribes residing in the north. Only four of every hundred churches were located in northern communities. In addition, though an estimated 2.3 million northern people had moved south to find work, there was not a single church where they could worship in their own language.

Historical View

The newcomers to southern Ghana are from forty different ethnic groups that have their own distinct languages and customs. Some move south to find temporary employment during the dry season when they are unable to raise crops at home. Others come looking for permanent work and greater opportunities. Because the northern peoples have an illiteracy rate of over 95 percent, the jobs they find in the south are menial and offer little hope of advancement.

While more developed than the north, southern Ghana suffers from extraordinarily high

Let My People Know... and Go

unemployment. Immigrants from the north have met with prejudice and resentment. In addition, many southern Ghanian Christians have held the misconception that the northerners were Muslims who were resistant to evangelistic efforts. Thus, few Christians in the south bothered to introduce their new neighbors from the north to Jesus Christ.

Establishing The Northern Outreach Programme

Some southern Christians now realize that most of their northern neighbors have combined elements of Islam with their own traditional beliefs and rituals. When moving south looking for a new life, they are open to new ideas and some are finding new life in Jesus Christ. God has awakened His people in Ghana, and the Presbyterian Church of Ghana has established the Northern Outreach Programme (NOP) to evangelize and plant churches among populations of northern peoples who move south. Since 1990, under the

Annual Northern Outreach Programme rally involving many different people groups *Photo by Judy Theriault*

Let My People Know... and Go

direction of the Rev. Solomon Sule-Saa, the outreach efforts have produced close to twenty new churches.

The NOP is an ambitious, holistic ministry. Their goal is to plant linguistically and culturally relevant churches in each of the forty northern ethnic groups. The NOP provides literacy classes and vocational training along with a winning witness for Jesus Christ and they envision new Christians returning to their northern villages with the Gospel. Their stated goal is "Literacy, Development and a Church for Every Northern People by the Year 2000." With your prayers, and God's help, the NOP can reach its goal.

Prayer Concerns

PLEASE PRAY without ceasing:
• Southern Muslims were the first to recognize the newcomers in their midst and they were working to befriend the immigrants and convert them to Islam. Some say that Muslims wanted to turn Ghana into an Islamic country by the year 2000. Pray that God will raise up thousands of Christians to demonstrate His

Their T-shirts proclaim the NOP goal

Photo by Judy Theriault

Let My People Know... and Go

love to Ghana's northern peoples and to introduce them to the only One who offers salvation.

- The NOP struggles with meager resources in the midst of overwhelming need. In the past, 90 percent of their funds have come through the PC(USA), mostly from the Frontier Mission Fund. Join the people of the NOP in prayer asking God to move the Christians of southern Ghana to support the ministry with both their donations and their time and talent. Pray also for more generous giving from PC(USA) people to enable the NOP to increase its outreach.
- Most of the NOP's work has been in Accra, the capital. They hope to have a national network of ministries all working to reach the northern peoples. Pray that many Christians in Takoradi, a seaport city with a large number of northerners, will be moved by God to active ministry to the foreigners in their midst.

Cars were especially fascinating for Solomon but, for the Mamprusi boy, they were also rare and out of reach...

The Mamprusi

Rev. Solomon Sule-Saa of Ghana

Photo by Judy Theriault

Let My People Know... and Go

The Mamprusi of Ghana, Africa

When young Solomon completed the highest level of education available in their village, his Muslim father sent him to live with a Christian uncle in order to be closer to another school. Solomon was a Muslim and had been warned to stay away from missionaries, but his uncle introduced him to one who had a car. Solomon liked to ride in cars. Soon he was regularly riding out into the countryside with the missionary who went to preach and teach about Jesus. Solomon had no intention of becoming a Christian; he just went along for the ride. But God had other plans. The Rev. Solomon Sule-Saa now directs the Presbyterian Church of Ghana's Northern Outreach Programme (NOP) and is working to reach his own people and dozens of others with the Gospel of Jesus Christ.

Who are the Mamprusi?

Like most of the other Northern tribes of Ghana, exposure to Christianity is a relatively new experience for the Mamprusi. The first missionaries arrived in 1940. This new Christian influence exists in the midst of several centuries of traditional ancestor worship and an allegiance to a strong chiefdom structure. The Mamprusi are one of four tribes who are descendants of the mythical "red hunter." The "Nayiri" is the paramount Mamprusi chief and the Frafra, Nabem, Talensi, and Kusai tribes are also subject to him. Traditional ancestor worship recognizes the supreme god Naa-wuni, the same name used for God by both Christians and Muslims. The Mamprusi have a historical devotion to Islam because

of old trade relations with Muslims which often included the appointment of a Muslim as a consultant in Nayiri's court. The Mamprusi celebrate Muslim festivals, but their spiritual allegiance to Islam is minimal. Eighty-two percent of the Mamprusi view themselves as followers of their own traditional religion, and it is estimated that only 14 percent are Muslim.

The Mamprusi people are primarily subsistence farmers and livestock producers. Of the 227,000 Mamprusi, it is believed that 10 percent have migrated to southern Ghana to seek employment or to escape parental control. The high rate of illiteracy (over 95 percent) has forced most to become servants or load carriers, or to take other low paying jobs.

Prayer Concerns

PLEASE PRAY without ceasing for:
- Solomon Sule-Saa, as he directs the outreach to the Mamprusi and other northern peoples. Pray for his family, his efforts at managing an ever increasing ministry, and his ability to love and provide for the northerners who have tremendous physical needs as well as great need for the Savior.
- continued work in Bible translation. Presently, only three chapters of Genesis and two chapters of Luke have been translated into Mamprusi.
- Mamprusi who relocate to southern Ghanian cities. They are vulnerable spiritually and economically. Pray that they meet caring Christians and find help for today and hope for eternity.
- continued resources and people to teach literacy classes and vocational classes in the Mamprusi language.
- the twenty Mamprusi believers who have come to faith in the south and who now worship with those from other ethnic groups. Pray that they will soon

have a church in their own language and that it will reach many of their people both in the south and in their homeland.

Vital Statistics

Religion   Traditional
Language   Mampruli

Population
    Mamprusi: 227,000
    Ghana*: 17,543,000

Christian Status
    (includes Protestants, Catholics, Orthodox)
    Mamprusi: 5%
    Ghana*: 64%

*Note: includes all people groups

"Do you have a Bible?" the worker asked, pulling the New Testament from his pocket...

The Kazaks

"No," the Kazak man responded.

Handing the man the Kazak translation of the New Testament, the worker asked another question, "Have you heard of Jesus?"

The man responded, "Is that another book?"

After seventy years of communist occupation and atheistic teachings, many Kazaks have never heard the name of Jesus. A climate of change, however, is settling over Kazakhstan.

Who are the Kazaks of Kazakhstan?

The hammer and sickle no longer flies over this new Central Asian Republic. In December 1991, Kazakhstan gained independence from the former Soviet Union. The country adopted a new flag, a new national anthem and instituted Kazak as the national language. They are pressing forward to find a new identity and to establish a stable lifestyle for themselves as individuals and as a body.

Let My People Know... and Go

Independence has arrived along with emotional and economic upheaval for the people. While they are overjoyed with their new-found freedom, there is an immediate price to pay. Famine, sickness, poverty and overall discouragement abound. Some people have expressed a desire to return to the stability of the former communist regime. Most people are willing to endure the hardship now, with the hope that a better day is soon coming.

Kazak woman selling refreshments at a tour bus stop

Photo by Bernice Condit

Let My People Know... and Go

The Kazaks, a warm and hospitable people, have been forced to contend with foreign rule for much of their history. Ghengis Khan aggressively marched into the region in the eleventh century and the Russians overtook the area in the eighteenth century. Currently Kazakhstan struggles with outside powers who have an economic interest in the country's natural resources.

Spiritual Security

Kazakhstan is also struggling to find spiritual security. Islam has lingered for centuries on the face of the culture but has not penetrated the hearts of the people. They say, "To be Kazak is to be Muslim," but in reality they practice a traditional religion, including ancestor worship. Many have succumbed to the atheism proclaimed by their former communist government.

The Presbyterian Church (USA) is supporting two couples in Kazakhstan, the Kims and the Woods-Hendersons. The Kims are actively ministering through music. The Woods-Hendersons are fervently working with The Revival Baptist Mission. Several Christian churches have been started in Kazakhstan, and, though the percentage of Kazak Christians is low, there is hope that the people will see that Christ is the One who will be the fulfillment of their new-found freedom.

The Kazak people are now able to choose how they will live and who they will be as individuals and as a nation. As they look to the world for answers to their questions, now is the time for Christians to step forward with the message of Jesus Christ. May they come to know His name and recognize Him as the source of their identity and security now and forever.

Prayer Concerns

PLEASE PRAY without ceasing for:

- healing of the Kazak land. Years of nuclear testing have destroyed entire regions and have had adverse effects on the inhabitants.
- peace and reconciliation between the Russified (urban) and Traditional (rural) Kazaks. In particular, there is great tension over the languages in which people choose to communicate (Russian versus Kazak).
- the integrity and wisdom of missionaries devising strategies on how best to minister to the Kazaks.
- the workers whom God will call to take the Gospel to the people in Kazakhstan, that they might respond with enthusiasm.

Vital Statistics

Religion   Islam, Traditional
Language   Kazak, Russian
Population   Kazakhstan: 17,206,000

Christian Status
     (includes Protestants, Catholics, Orthodox)
     Kazakhstan: 26.2%

The "white gold" of Uzbekistan has become a devastating "white plague."

The Uzbeks

Illustration by Ruth Elliott

The former USSR, hoping to compete in the international textile market, chose Uzbekistan for the site of their cotton plantations. Because the arid land was not suitable for cotton crops, water and land resources were manipulated to force fruitful harvests. The cotton, or "white gold," earned great sums of money for a time. Soil and water mismanagement, however, has left Uzbekistan with an ecological disaster, just one example of the many great challenges which face the new and emerging Central Asian republic.

Who are the Uzbeks of Uzbekistan?

Having proclaimed independence in September, 1991, the people of Uzbekistan are in the process of rebuilding their lives, reshaping their identity and rejuvenating their land. Under 70 years of Communist rule they sacrificed traditions, strengths and dreams, for the prosperity of the greater Soviet Union. Reestablishing their culture and restoring their land has proven to be a struggle.

Tension between the ethnic Uzbeks and the Russian people of Uzbekistan has been high. Many Uzbeks blame the Russians for the pains and "evils" they have experienced in their country. For the survival of the new nation there has been a renewed effort to make peace between the two people groups.

Uzbekistan, a secular state, has no official religion. Because the people are hungry for spiritual truth, many cults are emerging and capitalizing on this climate of openness and need. In addition, Muslims from Saudi Arabia, Turkey, Iran and Pakistan are eager to establish cultural and economic ties with the new republic in hopes of creating a common market of Islamic states.

Central Asia has Islamic roots which reach back many centuries. There has been a recent revival of Islam in the Uzbek capital, Tashkent, now known as the Islamic capital of Central Asia. Men and women are encouraged to wear traditional dress and the high morals of the faith are stressed. Islamic practices are of great cultural value to the youth, who are playing key roles in reforming and reclaiming the Uzbek identity.

God Alone Will Guide

A small percentage of the people living in Uzbekistan are Christians. Uzbeks and foreign nationals alike carry on the work of ministry. Due to the sensitive nature of Christian service in countries like Uzbekistan, details cannot be given regarding the lives of these people. Please hold them up in prayer, however, and ask God, who sees their situation, to guide and protect them.

In the midst of this extremely volatile atmosphere, may God work mightily, that the Uzbek people might come to know and follow Jesus Christ. He alone will be the trustworthy Guide and Healer of their peoples and land. He alone will complete their search for an identity and lead them to full restoration.

Prayer Concerns

PLEASE PRAY without ceasing for:
- a wide distribution and acceptance of the Uzbek translation of the New Testament, Genesis and Psalms, published in 1992.
- God to raise up Uzbek writers, composers and artists who will creatively present the Gospel to the people in traditionally appreciated forms.
- our Uzbek brothers and sisters, that they might be the people God intends them to be and find their place in the eternal Kingdom of God.

Vital Statistics

Religion	
Islam	
Language	
Uzbek, Russian	
Population	
Uzbekistan: 23,377,000	
Christian Status	
(includes Protestants, Catholics, Orthodox)	
Uzbekistan: 4.7%	

Cut off from friends and family for over forty years, the American Yup'iks boarded the plane for the first "Friendship Flight" into Russia since the Cold War had begun...

The Yup'ik

Over half of the passengers were elders from Gambell Presbyterian Church. Filled with "butterflies" of anticipation, they made the short, 25-mile flight over the Bering Strait. Landing in Providenya, they were greeted by Russians who had choreographed a traditional dance to a song they had learned from a radio broadcast originating in Nome, Alaska. The song was "Jesus Loves Me." Though many Yup'iks have been separated from the world and from each other, God has not forgotten them. Through their reunion, God is now calling them to walk together in Christ and to proclaim His name to their people and to the nations around them.

Who are the Yup'ik?

The Yup'ik people inhabit northeast Siberia, as well as St. Lawrence Island and western portions of Alaska. Shortly after World War II Stalin closed

the borders of the Soviet Union, separating extended families in Siberia and the USA. In 1988, under Gorbachev the borders were reopened.

Thought to be one of the oldest cultures in North

America, the Yup'ik of both Alaska and Siberia are a marine-based people who make their living hunting and fishing. They also herd reindeer and raise the Arctic fox. They have a rich history of folk singing, dancing and drumming, and come together on cold evenings to celebrate these talents. For centuries their people have withstood the harsh living conditions with grace, taming the rugged tundra and adapting to the extreme climate.

The Yup'ik live in a spiritually diverse climate. Shamanism has had a powerful influence among the people. There is a current movement on both sides of the Bering Strait to recapture this tribal religious form. The Russian Orthodox Church has a strong presence among the Siberian population, but has not focused on the native peoples.

A Change in Climate

Igor Pavlov, Director of Religion and Cultural Affairs of the Russian Magadan State, when visiting Alaska, was impressed with the positive impact the church was making on alcoholism, drug abuse and suicide. He invited the Presbyterian Church (USA) to establish a mission presence among the Yup'ik in Russia. Several denominations have come together to undertake this exciting endeavor. The resulting Chukotka Native Christian Ministry (CNCM) was formed in 1992. American Yup'iks are working closely with the government in the Chukotka region and have been eagerly received by the people.

There is a great warming trend occurring in the Russian Far East! God is reaching out to the Yup'iks with the help of their brothers and sisters from Alaska. The PC(USA) has enthusiastically channeled support through the Yukon Presbytery, eager to see churches established in the villages of Siberia. May the Yup'iks recognize Christ as their Lord and eternal

Savior, and look to Him today to heal and strengthen their land.

Yup'ik child   *Photo courtesy of Wycliffe Bible Translators, International*

Prayer Concerns

PLEASE PRAY without ceasing for:

- Timothy Gologergen and Howard Slwooko, native Yup'iks from St. Lawrence Island currently leading the CNCM ministry. Also, please pray for the protection of all Yup'iks and their leaders as they have experienced much spiritual attack.
- the medical and nutritional needs of the Russian Far East peoples.
- the Holy Spirit to move American Christian Yup'iks, especially youth, to consider mission work among the Siberian Yup'ik.

Vital Statistics

Religion
Russian Yup'ik: Shamanism
Alaskan Yup'ik: Christianity, Shamanism
Language
Russia: Siberian Yup'ik, Russian
Alaska: Yup'ik, English
Population
Yup'iks of Chukchi Region: 1,200
Russian Chukchi Region*: 157,000
Yup'iks of Alaska: 1,000
Alaska*: 550,000

*Note: includes all people groups

Mr. and Mrs. Oudom, natives of Laos, met Jesus Christ in Houston, Texas...

The Lao

They had flown from their country to visit their son, Bounchan, who was working as a pastor in the USA. To their great surprise, he introduced them to the God of the universe. Baptized in John Knox Presbyterian Church, they returned to Laos a year later to start a Christian fellowship in their village. Various conflicts with the government have made this endeavor quite stressful. However, the Oudoms have continued to tell people about Jesus Christ with an undying spirit, and the people of Laos are listening.

A History of Barriers

Laos is a country searching for stability and peace. They were immediately launched into civil war following independence from France in 1953. In 1975, the Communist forces gained control and remain in

Illustration by Ruth Elliott

Let My People Know... and Go

leadership today. According to the government, the country's greatest needs are in the areas of education, health and self-development.

The Lao people have followed Theravada Buddhism, mixed with animism, since 1375. It continues to be the national religion today with the approval of the communist government. For many, Buddhism has become part of their identity and has been integrated into their traditions and social structures. It is difficult for people to leave the Buddhist lifestyle, for in doing so they feel they will forsake their cultural heritage as well as their families.

Climbing Barriers

A small percentage of Laotian people became Christians through the ministry of the Swiss Brethren and Christian Missionary Alliance in the early 1900's. Until the point of the Communist takeover their Christian churches were growing. In 1975, however, Communist officials confiscated church property, closed down Christian schools and burned Bibles. Many Christians fled the country. The path for Laotian believers has not been easy, yet a remnant has remained and persisted in their faith. There are over 160 Christian fellowship groups meeting in Laos today.

The PC(USA) desires to support and encourage the Lao Christians. Through a Presbyterian frontier mission initiative in 1995 the denomination asked Rev. Bounchan Keomanikhot to serve as a part-time national consultant in Laotian ministries. Rev. Keomanikhot is the only Lao pastor in the PC(USA) and currently ministers at the First Presbyterian Church of Cornelia, Georgia. He has organized the Lao Presbyterian Council which facilitates outreach and Christian leadership training for Laotian people in the USA and in Laos. The PC(USA) has also cooperated with the Lao government to build and support a school in Nakoong Village. Through this educational effort, we hope to demonstrate that Christians are concerned about the emotional and physical welfare of the Laotian people, as well as their spiritual well-being.

Rev. Keomanikhot writes, "The rice fields are big and the servants are few... The world is just next door to us, therefore we should start the ministry right from the place that we are standing and go throughout the world." Will you and your church start the ministry from the place that you are standing and go throughout the world? Start with prayer and see where God will lead you. Join Rev. Keomanikhot in asking the Lord of the harvest to send out workers into the "rice" fields and beyond (Matthew 9:38). May all people, in Laos and across the globe, have the opportunity to hear that Jesus Christ is Lord and that He is our Savior.

Prayer Concerns

PLEASE PRAY without ceasing that:
- the church will grow along family lines, with entire families coming to Christ through a group decision.
- God will spur Lao Christians to pursue theological and pastoral training, that a firm Lao leadership will be established in the church.
- resources will be provided for Bibles and study materials.
- God will provide for the education and health care needs of the Laotian people.
- the Lao government will allow Christians to freely talk of their faith in Jesus Christ. Laotians are

Let My People Know... and Go

starving for the Gospel and listen intently when it is presented.
- the PC(USA) will carefully discern and follow God's will concerning their involvement in the Lao ministry.

Vital Statistics

Religion Theravada Buddhism Traditional
Language Lao
Population Laos*: 4,583,000 Lao in USA: 130,000
Christian Status (includes Protestants, Catholics, Orthodox) Laos*: 0.05% Lao in USA: 5%

*Note: includes all people groups

Pu Chan, a prophetic leader among the Wa, advised the men to saddle his pony and follow it until it stopped...

The Wa

Over numerous hills and through the valleys of Myanmar they followed their animal guide. Pu Chan said it would take them to a "white brother" who had the book of God. After two weeks of travel, the pony turned, walked through an open gate and, entering a small community, it stopped. The men were confused for they could see no one. Hearing noises from a hole in the ground by which the pony stood, they moved closer and peered down. Two blue eyes looked up at them and a voice boomed, "Hello, strangers." It was American missionary William Marcus Young. He was in the process of digging a well for the Lahu people, whom he had come to serve. "Do you have the book of God," Asked the Wa? "I do, " came the reply. The men, overcome with joy, asked the "white brother" to return with them immediately and explain the book to their people.

Unable to return with the Wa because of his ministry with the Lahu, Young and several Christians from the Karen tribe told the Wa men about Jesus Christ and trained them to teach their people about God and His Word. The new Christians soon returned to their tribe high in the mountains with the sought-after treasure in their hearts. The Gospel was thus planted among the Wa, but World War II and communist oppression slowed the spread of the good seed.

Recently several Christians from the Wa Hill Tribe hiked out, through the rugged mountains of

Myanmar, into Thailand in search of a missionary for their people. For nearly 100 years they have been praying for their own pastor to come and help them proclaim the Gospel. They feel their people are especially open to God at this crucial point in their history. Having experienced many years of oppression and poverty, as rebels against the socialist Burmese dictatorship, they are entering a new era seeking peace, seeking improvement, seeking truth. The Wa are eager for change.

Who are the Wa?

There are close to two million people in the Wa hill tribe. Approximately one half of them reside in Myanmar, while the remainder spread across the borders of neighboring Thailand and China. Their villages are located in the isolated hills of Southeast Asia and can be reached only by horse or on foot. As one of the most powerful hill tribes in Myanmar, the Wa are known for their military strength and pride. Until the early 1970's, they practiced headhunting and were greatly feared by outsiders.

Living in Myanmar

The Myanmar Communist Party had tight control over the Wa from 1967 to 1989. Under communist rule, the Wa territory became a war zone in which many soldiers were killed, disabled and fell prey to disease. As a result, there are many widows and orphans in their society today. In April, 1989, the Wa of Myanmar ousted the Communist Party from their territory and declared the United Wa State Party.

Presently the majority of the Wa are animists, worshipping and offering sacrifices to appease intimidating spirits. There is a widespread belief, even among non-Christians, that Jesus can help them and bring them new life. A few of the state officials

Wa woman surrounded by children

Photo by Beth Jacobson

Let My People Know... and Go

are Christians and are eager to develop evangelistic work among their people.

Church Involvement

God has opened doors in the last few years for American missionaries, Dave and Karen Eubank, to meet the Wa and work with their Christian leaders. Several people from Thailand and the USA, including Marcus Young, great grandson of William Marcus Young, are teaming with the Eubanks. They will join the Wa Christian Fellowship in their goal to see all of their people come to know Christ by the year 2000.

Prayer Concerns

PLEASE PRAY without ceasing for:
- God to continue raising up Christians from around the world and within Wa State to join in establishing churches among the Wa.
- a crop substitute for the illegal opium cash crop, as well as general agricultural development.

Woman smoking tobacco while harvesting opium
Photo by Beth Jacobson

Let My People Know... and Go

- medical care and the development of an educational system for the Wa children.
- protection of Christian Wa leaders from drug lords and hostile governmental officials.
- the Wa children living in the Christian home, supported by the PC(USA), in Chiang Mai, Thailand. Some families living in the remote border villages of Thailand and Myanmar send their children to live in this home and attend public school in the city. Pray that these youth will grow in their faith in Jesus Christ.

Vital Statistics

Religion	
Traditional	
Language	
Wa	
Population	
Wa: 2,000,000 (1,000,000 in Myanmar)	
Myanmar*: 46,275,000	
Christian Status	
(includes Protestants, Catholics, Orthodox)	
Wa: 2.5-3.0%	
Myanmar*: 6.5%	

*Note: includes all people groups

"Get out of my way Foul One!.."

The Dalits

"It's your duty to clean the latrine, not to get in my way!" growled Sharma, a Brahmin youth, at the Untouchable.

"Does it ever bother you that we treat them worse than our animals?" asked his friend Chauhan from the warrior class.

"Why no! That's just the way it is. You know the creation story as well as I do, Chauhan. God created people in four classes. He created my caste, the Brahmins, from his head. He created your class, the Kshatriyas, from his arms. He created the Vaishyas, the traders, from his thighs; and the Shudras, the servants, from his lowly feet. Those Untouchables weren't created from the body of God and so they are unworthy to be humans. Now come on, let's go. Watch

Young Dalit boy in prayer
Photo courtesy of Witnessing Ministries of Christ

Let My People Know... and Go

out! Don't let his shadow fall on you; you'll become unclean."

Who are the Dalits?

The Untouchables, or Dalits (an Indian term meaning one who is oppressed, downtrodden, or crushed) number 135 million. Scattered throughout India, they make up 15 percent of India's population. The Untouchables are an abused, despised, illiterate people who have been forced into wretchedness and grinding poverty by the caste system. The Untouchables have been denied respectable means of livelihood for centuries and are only allowed to do tasks deemed unclean by caste Hindus, such as latrine cleaning and disposing of dead animal carcasses. The Untouchables, considered to be below domesticated animals, are only allowed to have demeaning names like "ugly," "stupid," or "filthy." Because of their sorrow and oppression, the Untouchables are responding to Jesus Christ, who understands their suffering.

God is Moving

Presbyterian frontier mission supports the ministry of the Rev. Phil Prasad and the Witnessing Ministries of Christ (WMC) in the state of Uttar Pradesh. WMC is an exciting holistic ministry that has dedicated itself to reaching the Untouchables and founding a self-supporting Dalit church. While preaching the Gospel and planting churches, they also provide education, health care, economic development, and vocational training for the Untouchables, allowing them to escape the vicious trap of the Hindu caste system.

Let My People Know... and Go

The Dalits of India, Southern Asia

A congregation at a wedding ceremony in Isagarh
Photo courtesy of Witnessing Ministries of Christ

The Lord is moving! Through WMC's ministry, the
Dalit church has doubled in size over the past year and
an average of 1.6 new churches are started EACH day!
Opportunities like this don't repeat themselves very
often. Let us join with Witnessing Ministries of Christ
in completing their God-given vision of a self-
supporting Dalit church. The fields are ripe for the
harvest!

Prayer Concerns

PLEASE PRAY without ceasing that:
- the Dalits will continue coming to Christ in large
  numbers and that new believers will have missionary
  hearts for the "unreached" of India and the world.
- support will be provided for the salary, training and
  supplies (Bibles, hymnals, text books and bicycles)
  that the traveling pastors and elementary school
  teachers need. Each pastor is responsible for fifteen
  churches and visits three a day during the work
  week.
- the Lord will protect the pastors from attacks by
  those who do not want the Untouchables to have a
  religion or an education.
- the Lord will raise up churches to participate in the

Covenant Presbyteries Initiative through which Presbyterian congregations in the USA help to plant self-supporting presbyteries among the Dalit people in partnership with the Rural Presbyterian Church, India.

- the Lord will raise up sponsors to support 1000 Dalit children in the boarding school program.

Vital Statistics

Religion	
	Hindu
Language	
	Hindi
Population	
	Dalits: 135,450,000
	India*: 900,000,000
Christian Status	
	(includes Protestants, Catholics, Orthodox)
	Dalits: 21.0%
	India*: 2.61%

*Note: includes all people groups

The "Forgotten Land" is a label often applied to Albania...

The Albanians

In 1944, Communist strongman, Enver Hoxha, gained power and gradually severed almost all Albanian contacts with the outside world. He outlawed all religion, executing priests and bulldozing churches and Mosques. In their place he erected statues of himself in every community inscribed with the phrase "Glory Be to Hoxha." When Hoxha died in 1985, Albanians began to wake up to the fact that Hoxha had spirited away billions of dollars to Swiss bank accounts, leaving the country economically and spiritually destitute. A mission worker recently asked an Albanian college student, "What do you believe in?"

Albanian girls   *Photo by Tom Theriault*

Let My People Know... and Go

His reply, "I don't believe in anything. I used to believe in Hoxha; but now I know it was all a big lie." After the Gospel was briefly explained to him, the young Albanian responded with earnest longing, "I know I must make a decision soon; I can't go on much longer believing in nothing."

First to Receive the Gospel

Ironically, Albania was one of the first lands to receive the Gospel (according to Romans 15:19 Paul planted a church in Illyricum, ancient Albania). Eastern Orthodoxy held sway until the early fifteenth century, when the Ottoman Turks swept in with Islam. Five hundred years of persecution under Islam was followed by an even more ruthless suppression under Communism. Statistics are hard to confirm, but estimates are that prior to Hoxha, 70 percent of Albania's 3.3 million citizens were Muslim, 20 percent were Orthodox, and 10 percent Roman Catholic.

Let My People Know... and Go

Because of Hoxha's efforts to eliminate all religion, most Albanians, especially the younger generations, do not closely identify with any faith community. Recent missionary efforts have established tiny churches in the major cities. However, hundreds of remote towns and villages are still without any lasting witness to Christ. There seems to be a great openness to Christianity among Albanians of Muslim background who tended to stand with Christians against atheistic Communism.

Crossing Bridges

Presbyterian missionaries were among the first to venture into Albania when the iron curtain of isolation fell in 1990. We are endeavoring to work alongside the evangelistically-oriented Albanian Orthodox archbishop at the same time as we are reaching out to the unreached. There is some thought that newly reborn followers of Jesus among Albanian Muslims would be ideal missionaries to the much more traditional and resistant Albanian Muslim populations in neighboring Macedonia.

Praise God, who has not forgotten the beautiful people of Albania. Their day of salvation is dawning once again, and we American Presbyterians are among those through whom the Light is shining!

Prayer Concerns

PLEASE PRAY without ceasing for:
- the newly planted churches, characterized by vibrant faith and outreach, and for Spirit-filled Albanian leadership.
- expanded partnership and good relations between our Presbyterian workers and the Albanian Orthodox Church.
- the development of a strategy for reaching Albanian Muslims in neighboring countries.

Let My People Know... and Go

Vital Statistics

Religion	
Islam, Atheism	
Language	
Albanian	
Population	
Albania*: 3,521,000	
Christian Status	
(includes Protestants, Catholics, Orthodox)	
Albania*: 5%	

*Note: includes all people groups

"What? You're not going to bed...

The Kurds

It's only 2 a.m. Our guests only came yesterday.
There's so much to talk about. Did you hear, my
cousin's sister in London is engaged! Wish it were me.
Come, dance. We've been sitting on the mats drinking
tea and listening to the musicians for hours. Life is so
grim. How better to forget and remember our beloved
Kurdistan. From the beginning of time our ancestors
danced these steps to this music. This is what keeps us
Kurds. Sleep's for another time. I'm just going to dance
until I have to leave for the factory at seven."

Who are the Kurds?

Nearly 30 million
Kurds, probably the
Medes of the Bible,
comprise the world's
largest ethnic people
without a state of their
own. Concentrated in
Kurdistan which spans
parts of Turkey, Iraq, Iran
and Syria, millions spill
over into countries of
Central Asia, the Middle East, Europe and North
America.

Archaeology confirms that mountainous Kurdistan
cradled one of the earliest centers of cultural
development: agriculture and equipment, domesticated
animals, metallurgy, weaving, and fired pottery. Each
mountain valley sheltered a different Kurdish tribe,
independent kingdoms and city states. Mass migrations
in and out of Kurdistan characterize Kurdish history.

Throughout centuries stained with suffering, Kurds have demonstrated an unusual ability to absorb and adapt to other cultures.

Color distinguishes the Kurds in dress and the arts. Women's long skirts and blouses utilize brilliant velvets, silky synthetics, layer upon layer.

Partners for The Gospel

Ninety percent (nearly two million) of all Kurds living outside Kurdistan are in Germany. The Presbyterian Church (USA) partners with the German state church to share the love of Jesus Christ through proclamation and humanitarian services among the 40,000 Kurds living in Berlin. Many Kurdish "guest workers" and asylum seekers find in PC(USA) mission co-worker, Rev. Christine (Goodman) Callison, and her German colleague, Almut,

Kurds in Germany   *Photo courtesy of Presbyterian*
Frontier Fellowship

Let My People Know... and Go

Rev. Christine (Goodman) Callison in Germany
Photo courtesy of Presbyterian Frontier Fellowship

trusted friends and counselors. Flor, a new Kurdish
sister, partners in the weekly singing and worship
meetings, periodic concerts, dances, English camps, and
social and human rights services.

Prayer Concerns

PLEASE PRAY without ceasing for:
- the ministry to Kurds in Iraq, which the PC(USA)
  also supports.
- the elimination of prejudice and discrimination
  against the Kurds in Germany and Iraq and
  throughout the world.
- the completion of Bible translations in three major

dialects: *Kurmanji, Lorani and Zaza (Dimili)*. The Gospel of Luke is now in the hands of 100,000 Kurds. Christian literature, drama and music are sorely needed via print, audio and video media.

- communities of Kurdish believers in Germany (several testify to the transformation Christ has made in their lives) and in Iraq (there are over a dozen followers of Jesus in a mutually led discipleship program).
- an increase in small businesses which aid in the self-development of impoverished Kurdish families (sheep-raising, computer and business training and management).
- Greg and Chris Callison, married in September, 1995. Greg is joining Chris in Berlin. Please pray that God will bless their marriage and minister through their lives among the Kurds.

Vital Statistics

Religion
Islam

Language
Kurmanji, Lorani, Zaza

Population
Total Kurdish Pop.: 25,910,000
Kurds in Germany: 2,000,000
Germany*: 80,000,000

Christian Status
(includes Protestants, Catholics, Orthodox)
Kurds in Germany: <1.0%
Germany*: approximately 75.8%

*Note: includes all people groups

Imagine waking up to a sky
blackened with ashes...

The Zoque

In the distance a volcano rumbles to life. Gathering
a few valuables, you flee your tribal home, never to
return again.

In 1982, the Chiconal
Volcano erupted, forcing
35,000 Zoque Indians to
abandon their villages.
Relocated by the Mexican
government, the farms and
adobe huts of the Zoque now
lie scattered throughout the
state of Chiapas in
Southeastern Mexico.

Culture

Using primitive agricultural methods, the Zoque
grow maize, beans, and squash to support themselves.
Spiritually, they practice a mix of Catholicism and
traditional rituals. Zoque Christians have undergone
persecution as a result of their faith in Jesus Christ.
Many have suffered damage to their property and
their lives have been threatened. Despite this
hardship, the seeds of the Gospel continue to be sown,
and slowly, the people are coming to know their
Savior. Approximately 5 percent of the Zoque are
Christians. There are six established churches and
they hope to be self-supporting in the near future.

God's Work Among the Zoque

Through the "Commitment to Share Good News," a
ministry of the Presbyterian Church (USA),

Let My People Know... and Go

Westminster Presbyterian and First Presbyterian Churches of Yakima, Washington are reaching out to the Zoque. Members of both churches have made many trips to Mexico to serve the people and support the established Zoque fellowships.

Merilee Buehler of Westminster Presbyterian Church speaks enthusiastically of the relationship her church has with the Zoque. She says, "If you want to experience life... If you want to experience growth... If you want to experience excitement, this is where it's at!" The Zoque partnership has proven to be one of the most energizing endeavors these congregations have

A team from Yakima visits the Zoque

Photo by Linda Markee

Let My People Know... and Go

known. Through time, energy, resources and prayer, the people of Yakima, Washington are making eternal investments in the Kingdom of God. Will you join them?

Prayer Concerns

PLEASE PRAY without ceasing that:
- effective strategies will be developed in using the "Jesus Film," which has recently been translated into the Zoque language. Pray that the Holy Spirit will bless these efforts.
- Sunday school teachers will receive needed training, and that Sunday school materials will be provided for the children.
- health care and nutrition for the Zoque children will improve.
- the new church construction project will progress smoothly and that workers will remain safe.
- Christians will reach out to the young Zoque men seeking jobs in town .

Vital Statistics

Religion
Traditional
Language
Zoque, Spanish
Population
Zoque: 35,000
Mexico*: 97,967,000
Christian Status
(includes Protestants, Catholics, Orthodox)
Zoque: 5.0%
Mexico*: 92.7% (5.2% are Protestant)

*Note: includes all people groups

Let My People Know... and Go

The Word And The World Bible Study
The GO in the KNOW

Introduction

Presbyterians have long believed that the Bible is the Word of God; it is the mind and heart of God made readable. The Bible is a gripping drama which lifts the curtain on the heart and mind of God, allowing us to see God in action and even to participate as energized actors in that drama. So what's on God's mind, and what is at the center of His heart? The following six studies (scenes in the drama) will attempt to sketch out what many consider to be the connecting theme, the heartbeat, of the divine-human story.

In short, we see the suspense-filled plot of the Bible to be the unfolding plan of God to reclaim His fallen world by planting an outpost of His Kingdom (obedient followers) in every human grouping, in every ethnic-tribal-language group, so that all may have opportunity to see and hear and respond to His saving love in their own language and culture. And He plans to do this with or without the cooperation of His covenant people. If His people play their part, all is well, and the unreached "nations" and God's already saved saints, are blessed. If God's chosen people horde the blessings of salvation, then those blessings are forcefully removed and exported to the "nations."

Judge for yourself: does this simple, saving theme— God's Missionary Heart and Purpose—expose the natural flow of the Biblical narrative, the inner coherence that we would expect in any good story? If ours is a God on the GO, then what does that mean for those who seek to KNOW and follow Him? We **pray** that these six studies will illuminate for you something of the heart and mind of God and will open new understandings regarding His WORD for the WORLD.

NOTE: We hope these studies can be used in a wide variety of settings to help God's Presbyterian people grasp more strongly the centrality and urgency of God's mission mandate. We hope they can be of inspiration *in personal devotions, in enrichment studies for sessions, deacons, women's circles, youth groups, home fellowship groups ... let your imagination soar!*

SCENE 1 — Prologue

Getting to KNOW

1. Genesis 1:1-5 (and 6-25 if desired) — What do we discover about God?

• List aspects of God's character that appear in this opening scene of the Bible.

• "God created the heavens and the earth ." Notice that the Bible does not begin with God creating a garden for His people nor does it begin with God's selection of His covenant people. What significance might be attached to this fact? What do we learn in this phrase about the thrust of God's creative energy, about the stage on which His creative love is to operate.

2. Genesis 1:26-28 — What do we discover about humankind?

• List aspects of our character that emerge in our first appearance on the divine/human stage.

• "Be fruitful and multiply and fill the earth." Fill the earth with what? If we are created to express God's "image" (to reflect God's character), could it be that we are commissioned with the task of multiplying His character? And what is the stage on which we are to express or export that image? Notice that we are made not to "fill" our garden, but to "fill the earth." What might that say about the nature of human fulfillment? Is there a missionary job description written into the very essence of the human heart — i.e. we will find fulfillment only as we reflect and project God's character all around the earth??

3. Genesis 3:1-5 and 24 — What do we discover about our predicament?
    • What is at the heart of human sin? Why did our first parents disobey their loving Creator?
    • What are the effects of human sin? Look both at the horizontal effects (on the human-to-human level) and the vertical effects (between God and humans). How are those effects prevalent today?

4. Genesis 11:1-9 — What do we discover about the beginnings of God's Plan to reclaim His lost loved ones?
    • What was the sin of the builders of Babel? Note the phrase "let us make a name for ourselves."
    • God acted in a Masterstroke of Mercy (to protect the earth from this conspiracy of "we can run things without God") and in a Masterstroke of Mission Strategy. How could dividing the world into language groups be the first step in God's Plan to win the world back to Himself?

SCENE 2 — The Plan Launched

Getting on the GO

1. Genesis 12:1-4 — A Family for All Families
Out of all the family/clan groupings listed in Genesis 10 and 11 God chose one small family. For what

purpose?

• God commanded Abram and clan to GO. Why do you think the command was stated three times ("from your country," "your kindred" and "your father's house")?

• What promises did God issue to Abram and clan and why were these meaningful to them?

• What was the underlying PURPOSE in the issuing of these promises — "and in you all the families (the ethnic groupings) of the earth shall be blessed"?

• The rest of the Bible answers the foundational question: "did they, or didn't they?" Did God's Covenant People export the blessings of covenant life to all the families (ethnic groupings) of the world or did God's Covenant People horde those blessings?

2. Note the reissuing of the promise-purpose covenant to Abraham's descendants —
  • to Isaac - Genesis 22:18
  • to Jacob - 28:14-15
  • Re-read the famous story of Joseph in Egypt from the vantage point of this promise-purpose covenant. Could it be that Jacob's obsession with getting "More and More for Me and Mine" (the M&M Syndrome) blinded him to God's love for the unreached surrounding nations, forcing God to expel the covenant blessings via Jacob's favorite son?? Notice that Joseph becomes an eloquent missionary spokesman to the unevangelized Egyptian monarch (Gen. 41:25- 32).

3. Re-read what is perhaps the pivotal scene in all the Old Covenant - the Exodus story.
  • Why did God deliver His people? Was it simply to extricate them from a tight and unpleasant spot? Note Exodus 7:5; 8:10, 19, 22; 9:14-16 for the wider, mission setting for this part of the drama.

• In the Central Celebration of Israel, the Passover, notice that there was to be room for the "alien," for those from the nations who respond to God's Covenant love (Exodus 12:47-49). What does this imply about the central celebrations of God's present-day people — is there room for the "nations" in our Christmas or Easter holidays, or are they pretty much "M&M" events??

4. God assigned to His Covenant People the thrilling role of displaying His name (i.e. His character) before all the distinct ethnic groupings of the world so that all would have a chance to believe and become part of the expanding covenant community. This was the job of the First Family of Faith. How about your family of faith? To what extent are you exporting the Good News to all the unevangelized peoples?

SCENE 3 — The Plan Lost

The GO and the Judges

1. The era of conquering the land proved to be a very dark period summed up at the end of the Book of Judges 21:25. Although there were some bright spots during these centuries (Deborah and Gideon), the overall tone was what??

2. The brightest spot of all warranted a whole Book — the Book of Ruth.
• Ruth 1:1-5 — Why did these upstanding Jews end up in the lowstanding land of Moab? Can you see God's Purpose for the nations at work in these unhappy events?

• Ruth 1:15 — Viewed from the mission perspective, how do these famous words fit into and reflect God's Plan for the nations?

• Ruth 4:18-22 — Look at where this pagan woman fits into God's eternal plans!!

Could it be fairly stated that this marvelous story is really a missions story — exposing God's heart for the unreached Moabite people group??

The GO and the Kings

3. Who was Israel's most famous King? What was his most famous exploit? What was the larger Purpose at work in that exploit?? Let's look again at that much-loved story of David and Goliath, found in 1 Samuel 17:41-47.

• Why did God deliver His Covenant people from their tight, dangerous spot? "That all the earth may know that there is a God in Israel" is perhaps the larger frame of reference into which this memorable story fits.

• As with the Exodus, God desires to deliver His Covenant people — but WHY?? What is the larger Purpose that underlies God's delivering love? How does that connect with God's Purpose for us that came through in Genesis 1:28?

4. Who was Israel's most prosperous King? What was his most notable achievement? Let's look again at the heartbeat that pulses through the Sanctuary of Israel — 1 Kings 8:41-43.

• There are seven petitions in the prayer with which Solomon dedicated the magnificent Temple. Notice that the center petition concerns not Israel's legitimate needs for help, but concerns the rightful

place of the "foreigner" in the Sanctuary, in the regular worship life of God's people.
   • How much room is there in your regular worship life and in the life of your congregation for the needs of the nations, and particularly for the ethnic groups which have not yet found their rightful place in the new Temple, the church??

SCENE 4 — The Plan Lost (Part II)

When Solomon died, the Kingdom was split, and for hundreds of years, God's Covenant People were consumed with their "M&M" concerns — with property and pleasures, not with the peoples of the world.

The Pleading of the Prophets

1. They lift high the Plan
   • Isaiah 2:1-4 — Notice the come and the go of the plan. What is the highest good of every nation? What must precede the establishment of world peace?
   • Isaiah 49:3 and 6 — What is the highest calling of God's Covenant people?

2. They decry Israel's abandonment of the Plan
   • Amos 4:1-2 — What concerns are God's Covenant People majoring in?
   • Ezekiel 5:5-15 — Israel's injustices and immoralities disgraced God's character (His name) among the nations and God had to take action to preserve that witness.

3. Why the horrendous disaster of the Exile??
   • Daniel 1:1-7 — When Israel hoarded its

Covenant blessings, what was the result?

 • Daniel in the lion's den and what did he do?? Read Daniel 6 again with the larger Purpose of God in mind. Was Daniel not a gifted missionary, sent to the unreached nations in the east to witness in word and deed to the living God? How successful was he?

 • Jeremiah 33:6-9 — God promised to restore His Covenant People, but for what larger Purpose? God desires to restore our lives, our families, our church. Why? His love for us grows best when it is expressed in the direction God lays out. And what is that larger Purpose and direction??

4. What is the sober warning to God's Covenant People today that was played out in ancient Israel?

THE PLAN RENEWED!

SCENE 5 — A Messiah for WHOM??

Getting to KNOW Him

1. Let's look into Matthew's portrayal of Israel's long-awaited Deliverer. What did God's Covenant people expect their Messiah would do?

 • Matthew 2:1-11 — According to Matthew, who were the first to recognize and bow the knee to the newborn Jewish Messiah?

 • Matthew 8:1-10 — Who were the first healed by Israel's Deliverer (note the vexing verse 10)!

 • Matthew 27:53-54 — Who were the first to properly identify the newly reborn Jewish Messiah?

 • What point might Matthew have been trying to make to his Jewish audience regarding the larger Purpose underlying the Messiah's ministry?

Whom is this Messiah for??

• Matthew 24:14 — According to Jesus, what must happen before He returns and makes all things new? Note that the word "nations" is "ethne" in Greek, which is equivalent to "all families" of Genesis 12:3. What urgency might this inject into the mission mandate?

2. How about Dr. Luke's script for the Messiah? Jesus runs into a buzz saw of biases when He returns home after his first hugely successful ministry tour. Pick it up in Luke 4: 14-30.

• How did his hometown audience receive the first installment of His mission message? (verse 22)

• What did Jesus hear between the lines in their response recorded in verse 23?

• What kind of people did Jesus cite in his reply (verses 24-28)?

• Why did this incite such fury among the hometown believers?

• What common debate is being replayed here — could it be the tug-of-war between a "home-confined faith" and Jesus' "worldwide ministry?" How does this debate play out in your faith community?

3. What's the one verse that every Sunday School alum can recite? Reconsider John 3:16 from the standpoint of God's Plan and Purpose. What does it say about God's heart and mind. And we must not forget John 3:36 — What are the consequences awaiting those who do not believe in Christ?

4. The story continues — Acts 1:1-8 — what "Jesus began to do and teach" was to be re-run in the lives of His followers. What direction is our faith walk to be heading as we follow this Messiah?

Let My People Know... and Go
Appendix A-9

SCENE 6 — A Church for WHOM??

Getting to GO with Him

Will we or won't we? Will we sit and soak in the blessings of abundant life in Christ or will we go with Him to the ends of the earth? That is the question which has confronted Christians from the get-go.

1. Acts 10:1-14, 34-45 — The conversion of Cornelius AND Peter!

• How did Peter react to the prospect of taking the Gospel of salvation in Christ to the Gentiles? Why did he react this way?

• What did it take to blast Peter out of his "home-confined faith?"

2. Let's take another look at some of Paul's most famous epistles, letters which have most often been hijacked and held captive to the musings of theologians. Remember, what was Paul, first and last??

• Romans 1:5, 16 and 15:23-24 — Why was Paul writing to the fat-cat Christians in Rome? Was it simply to build up their faith? (Note the verb in 15:24 "to be sent by you" means to "outfit me with provisions necessary for my journey.") Could the Book of Romans, usually regarded as a towering theological treatise, also be viewed as a missionary support letter??

• Ephesians — This elegant letter is often heralded as "the church epistle." What was the animating obsession of Paul's pen?

Read 1:10,22 — what is Paul's controlling vision?

Read 2:14-16 — what is the reconciling result of the "salvation by grace through faith" doctrine?

Read 3:5-9 — what is the riveting mystery that

Paul is so compelled to reveal?

Could Ephesians, commonly read as a challenge to the Body of Christ, also be a letter designed to launch that church into worldwide mission??

3. Final things — the grand finale
  • Revelation 7:9-10 — what is the goal towards which the church is to be pressing?
  • Revelation 22:1-2 — what is the last scene depicted? Who are the recipients of the healing balm?

Where does the healing stream come from? What does this suggest about the role to be played by the followers of the Lamb?

Epilogue

The Word of God has taken us deep into the heart and mind of God. From the opening lines of the drama to its grand finale, where is the healing, redeeming, creative and recreating love of God in Christ heading? And what role is God's Covenant People assigned in this saving drama? What happens when God's people decline that role? Is not God's Word for the World?

Paul clinches his case: "But how are they to call upon One in whom they have not believed? And how are they to believe in One of whom they have never heard? And how are they to hear without someone to proclaim Him?" Then Paul knits together the Old and New Covenants by quoting the great prophet Isaiah: "How beautiful are the feet of those who bring [this] good news!" (Romans 10:14-15).

Oh that Presbyterians might be on the GO with that Good News as never before! What might our Worldwide Savior be saying to you, to your family, to your congregation about the role He has scripted for you

Let My People Know... and Go
Appendix A-11

to play in the ongoing drama of the ages? Would your fellowship group or your congregation be ready to step out in world-class faith to adopt one of the unreached people groups that still has no winning witness to Christ?

God's very best to you as you give your very best to Him and to His global purposes.

Rev. Tom Theriault
Mission Pastor,
Solana Beach Presbyterian Church
Solana Beach, CA

Stepping Out—
An Invitation to Get Involved

If you, your church, or your small group is interested in becoming involved with a particular people group through prayer, in person and/or through your pocketbook, there are several ways to start.

...And once you've taken the first step, who knows where God will lead you!

FIRST STEP OPTIONS:

1. One-Time/Short-Term

a. Prayer: more detailed information is available on particular people groups to enable you to pray more specifically. See VALUABLE FRONTIER MISSION CONTACTS below.

b. Financial Giving
- Make check payable to PC(USA)
- Designate on check "Extra Commitment Opportunity #863001." Account #863001 is the PC(USA) Frontier Mission Fund.
- Designate, in a cover letter, name and location of people group to which you want to give.
- Send check and letter to: PC(USA) Central Receiving Service, 100 Witherspoon St., Louisville, KY 40202-1396, or to the presbytery receiving site in your area.
- Send copy of cover letter to: Rev. Jefferson Ritchie, PC(USA), International Evangelism, 100 Witherspoon St., Louisville, KY 40202-1396
-OR-

2. Long-Term

Through the PC(USA) "Commitment to Share Good News" Program, you can make a long-term commitment to a particular people group. (brochure available)

a. Prayer: until a church is established and mobilized within the culture to reach the remaining people in that culture. *God might lead you to do more!*

b. Going in person

c. Financial Giving

d. ???????

Please contact the Presbyterian Center for Mission Studies (listed below) if you are interested in taking one of the above steps. We will be glad to help you in that process.

VALUABLE FRONTIER MISSION CONTACTS

The Presbyterian Center for Mission Studies (PCMS): providing resources, motivating congregations and working closely with PFF and the Presbyterian Church (USA) to further frontier mission efforts. Located on the campus of the US Center for World Mission in Pasadena, CA.

Southern CA:	Jennifer Pratt	(818) 398-2468
	Judy Theriault	
	1605 E. Elizabeth St.	
	Pasadena, CA 91104	
	e-mail: pcms.parti@ecunet.org	

Presbyterian Frontier Fellowship (PFF): a Validated Mission Support Group of the Presbyterian Church (USA). Working to mobilize the PC(USA) for frontier mission.

Portland, OR:	Rev. Harold Kurtz	(503) 289-1865
	6146 N. Kerby Ave.	
	Portland, OR 97217	

Seattle, WA:	Rev. Dave Hackett	(800) 720-4PFF
	14512 NE 4th St.	
	Bellevue, WA 98007	

and
Kathy Giske   (206) 481-2707
5616 NE 199th Pl.
Seattle, WA 98155

Bethlehem, PA: Rev. Mark Southard (610) 861-9454
826 Clewell St.
Bethlehem, PA 18015

Birmingham, AL: Rev. Cody Watson   (205) 733-0390
2031-B Longleaf Dr.
Birmingham, AL 35216

Website: http://www.cyberspace.com/~hackett/pff/

The Worldwide Ministries Division of the Presbyterian Church (USA): supporting frontier mission throughout the world, that all peoples may know Christ and have a viable church in their midst.

Louisville, KY: Rev. Jefferson Ritchie (502) 569-5253
Ruth Daniels
100 Witherspoon St.
Louisville, KY 40202

Contact one of the above offices for regular updates on the growing Presbyterian frontier mission movement. Information is available on the eighty least evangelized people groups with which we are ministering. Perhaps you and your church can help to broaden the reach of the PC(USA) as we carry the Gospel to the unreached peoples of the world, for the glory of God.

"...I tell you, open your eyes and look at the fields! They are ripe for harvest." Jesus in John 4:35

Let My People Know... and Go
Appendix B-3

Bibliography

The information provided in our writings has been gathered on location by personnel of the Presbyterian Church (USA) and Wycliffe Bible Translators, International. Information has also been gathered on-site by staff members of the Presbyterian Center for Mission Studies and Presbyterian Frontier Fellowship.

In addition, the following resources were helpful in our research and writing.

Books and Articles

Grimes, Barbara G., ed. *Ethnologue: Languages of the World*. 12th ed. Dallas: Summer Institute of Linguistics, Inc., 1992.

Johnstone, Patrick. *Operation World*. Grand Rapids: Zondervan, 1993.

Rodgers, Mary M., Tom Streissguth, Colleen Sexton, ed. *Uzbekistan*. Minneapolis: Lerner Publications Company, 1993.

Wasilewska, Ewa. "Searching for Identity: The Independent States of Central Asia (Part One)." *The World and I* (June 1995): 249-259.

Wasilewska, Ewa. "The Forgotten Land: The Independent States of Central Asia (Part Two)." *The World and I* (July 1995): 188-201.

Wasilewska, Ewa. "Galloping Through Time: The Independent States of Central Asia (Part Three)." *The World and I* (August 1995): 210-221.

Selected People Profiles

Adopt-A-People Clearinghouse, Colorado Springs, CO.